EVERYDAY
Use

A Collection of Poetry and Prose

Volume I

Donna Reed

iUniverse, Inc.

New York   Bloomington

EVERYDAY USE

A Collecton of Poetry and Prose

iUniverse books may be ordered through booksellers or by contacting:
iUniverse
1663 Liberty Drive
Bloomington, IN 47403
www.iuniverse.com
1-800-Authors (1-800-288-4677)

ISBN: 978-1-4502-2811-4 (pbk)
ISBN: 978-1-4502-2812-1 (ebk)

Printed in the United States of America
iUniverse rev. date: 6/11/10

*This One is for
My Traveling Man*

Acknowledgments

I celebrate with gratitude every aspect of my life and all those who helped make this project possible. I owe a debt of gratitude to Shanny Burge and Cassandra Turner who reviewed this piece of work. Your comments were invaluable in bringing this collection to its final form. Thank you Ed Myers for designing my book cover. To Terry for pushing me to the end. You are truly my soul mate. To Norma for being the epitome of a mother. To Erreka and Erin for being my inspiration. And to O.V. and Treva for being there when I needed you. Last but not least, to Jesus Christ, my Savior for giving me guidance. I know his everlasting arms are around me. All power belongs to Him.

Contents

Introduction

As we voyage through this life experiencing different things, feeling different ways, and interpreting those experiences, we try in some way to make sense of it. You see, life has a way of taking us down roads we never anticipate on traveling. Everything that has happen to us since birth has made us who we are today. That's what Everyday Use is, a collection of poetry and prose about the issues we are dealing with in our lives every day. But the life challenges we face come to make us better human beings. Our life struggles portray our strengths and weaknesses. They cause us to soul search – to find out who we are and what our purpose in life. We should all embrace change because life is essentially a learning experience. By doing so, we are afforded a different perspective, thus allowing us to think more clearly about difficult or perplexing events and emotions.

Everyday Use thrives to show you human behavior and the social environment in narrative verse. Embracing a wide variety of subjects, this collection spans over many years and it narrates incidents, experiences, people, and things that have touched my heart. These are my thoughts and my hand and the space and the emotions at the time that I was writing. I hope to inspire readers of all ages and to make sense of this world in which we live.

Poetry
&
Prose

Donna Reed

When I See My Brother

When I see my brother walking down the streets,
he often looks confused but yet so very meek.
I can see in his eyes he is full of shame,
but he walks proudly by as though life is not a strain.
I look at his clothes and they are old and too small,
but I understand life events have caused him to fall.
Without question, I do know it is not all of his fault,
for the system has certainly contributed to his assault.

When I see my brother working hard every day,
he tries to reach his goal but something stands in his way.
I can see in his eyes the tiredness and frustration,
but he keeps holding on in hopes of restoration.
I say to myself he too is not to blame,
if only this world will treat everyone the same.
Yet he continues to work holding on to his dignity,
but again social structures have limited his ability.

When I see my brother who is standing in line,
his business suit is fitted and his shoes are shined.
But when I look into his eyes he cannot look back at me,
for he too is caught up in a polluted sea.
I tell myself here is a man who is the jack-of-all-trades,
but I cannot be fooled because it is only a masquerade.
Again I say to myself the system has him banned,
just like the poor man whom society says is not a man.

The Girl from Harriman Tennessee

Childhood comes and goes.
Before you know it, we are all grown up.
June to August, you were my childhood friend.
At a time I cried and yearn to go home,
you stepped in and filled the void.
You made me giggle like the happy child
playing with the little girl next door.

Oh, we had so much fun!
Just you and I walking the streets and alleys.
From playing horseshoe in the park to
walking back up the steep hill from the corner store.
From up on the hill to Mayberry Street.
There you found us hanging out together
like two birds of a feather.

The days were unending and hot.
But we made time short-lived laughing and
talking about everyone and each other.
Soon all of the fun ended.
We grew up and went our separate ways.
No more long summer days in Harriman.
No more hanging out with my summer buddy.

You made me smile when I was feeling sad.
You made me laugh while
I was thinking of my mama.
Your humorous spirit enlightened my world.
You filled my summer vacations
with nothing more than happy
childhood memories.

A Musical Genius

A Note to Stevie

I grew up on you Stevie.
Every house party you were there.
Every album my mama bought.
When no one was around, I listened
while reading the words on the back
and inside cover. I read and listened
enough to memorize every
word, pitch, and hum.
And no one could beat me sanging
your meaningful songs.

I grew up on you Stevie.
I am still grooving to the beat of:
Fingertips, Uptight, and Blowin in the Wind.
I am still clapping to Higher Ground
and Jesus Children of America.
You influenced my life four decades.
Now I watch my daughters sit and groove
to the melody of Master Blaster (Jammin).
I see them looking at the words to the songs.
I remember doing the same when I was young.

Thank you Stevie – thanks so much
for inspiring and lifting up my spirit.
You are a musical genius!
Thank you for touching my soul.
Your exceptional and creative power
had to be a gift from God.
I am so glad I grew up on your music.
Music wrapped in nothing but love!
Something shared and passed down
through many generations.

Black Folks

Black folks are nice people, sweet as can be.
Beautiful people with a great big heart.
Though they have little or nothing at all,
they will help and share with anybody.

Black folks are smart and creative too.
Name something they cannot do.
If only they were given the credit
for the many inventions they created.

They make the best of any situation.
Even during slavery, they were able to smile,
sing, and teach themselves to read and write.
Yeah, a resilient people–always getting back up!

And if you want some good old fashion cooking,
look for the hole in the wall restaurant or café
in any city or town. Those black folks will make you
hurt yourself eating their finger-licking soul food.

Black folks are nice people, sweet as can be.
They understand the world in which they live,
while others choose to look the other way.
That too is okay because black folks are
forgiving people full of compassion and grace.

A Purpose

It was all for a purpose. A purpose she did not see.
At the time, it was hard for her to understand.
But she endured until the very end.

He gave her hand on experience. On welfare and
food stamps and wore the shame mask quite well,
as she received monthly, a minimum of one sixty five.

Although her babies had different bloodlines,
she taught them to believe otherwise. She was the
soul provider and made sure they would all survive.

Once hungry and saw no means of food.
Lights turned off on the coldest winter day.
Didn't have enough loose coins to travel to and fro.

She walked for miles to the daycare and bus stop.
By the time she left home early mornings,
darkness greeted the evenings just the same.

Her spirit was broken and she was left alone to
understand the human race and all of its craziness.
She saw the poor and suffering & felt the same pain inside.

Where are the fathers she asked herself?
On Wall Street or on the job making minimum wages.
Statistics say they are sitting behind prison bars.

It was all for a purpose. A purpose she now understands.
Had she not experienced it, her life would not be the same.
It was all for a reason, a reason destined to be.

A Rising Star

She was a rising star–opening up and
making herself known to heaven and earth.
But as she planted herself on solid ground,
paradise welcomed her young soul to glory bound.

She was a rising star–so talented–so beautiful.
Hit after hit, she landed on her feet.
Her consistency made her who she was,
it took her where she wanted to be.

She was a rising star not knowing her destiny.
But none of us know what the future holds.
Sometimes the journey is short and wide.
Other times it is long and narrow.

She was a rising star–her life was not in vain.
While she was here–she danced the night away.
With certainty, she has left an indelible impression,
a prominent mark in music history.

In Loving Memory of Aaliyah

Breaking the Rules

She was pompous. He was practically homeless.
She was educated. He barely got through high school.
It was her they gave the job.
It was him they overlooked.
But sometimes you have to break the rules
because it is necessary that you do.

He visited her when she was ailing on her sick bed.
He caressed her face as she drifted off to sleep.
He scratched the dandruffs from her scalp
as she laid her head upon his lap.
He saw her at her worst: uncombed hair,
no make-up or designer suit. He saw her.

Every day he told her she was beautiful.
She was grateful for this man
whom she really did not know.
She realized he might not have a degree,
fancy car, or eminent job, but he was
the man who was there for her.

Sometimes you have to break the rules
and guidelines you have established.
It is essential that you do.
She embraced that man who nursed
her back to health. A man she may not
have accepted had she not taken ill.

Coming Up Short

We live in this oblivious world
pretending for so long until
we know no other way to think.
We search for something bigger,
something better.
We look in all the wrong places.
And we wonder why we keep
coming up short.

Donna Reed

A Beautiful Child

When I first met you,
I could not help but smile as I asked,
"Who is this beautiful child?"
You smiled too
and gave me a hug.
It was special
just as it was to your mom
the day you were born.

Enjoying our fellowship,
I noticed you was an independent
little thang and very smart too!
I just shook my head and said,
"God bless this beautiful child."
Not only did you have such a pretty face,
but a delightful spirit as well.
Who would not be proud of you!

So as you grow and develop
into a beautiful young lady.
Please remember you are unique,
characteristics within and about you
make you one of a kind.
Always love and be good-hearted
to yourself. And never reject who you are.
Because you are undeniably a beautiful child!

Death Row

No one wants to die.
Not even the man who bombed
the Oklahoma City Federal Building.

And those who say they do,
have either two reasons for saying so:
Hopelessness and Death Row.

Decade of Changes

Our hearts broken over the slaying of Malcolm and Martin.
The Black Panthers and the NAACP still gathering,
but one could only hear the echoes.
The Vietnam War was over,
but the country was still a little unsettling.
Military men coming home wounded and tormented.
All they could hear was the name, Charlie, and perhaps ran.

Black families welcomed the seventies.
Black men entered the manufacturing boom
working on jobs paying ten to fifteen dollars an hour.
Black families buying homes, cars, and more children entering college.
Black men were now able to take care of their families.
They were finally getting a taste of living
the American dream.

Something began to happen as the decade ended.
Deindustrialization-forcing black workers out of the labor force.
Leaving many of them discouraged and economically stressed.
Black daddies feeling less than a man
and walking away from their families.
Black mamas left to carry the load.
The eighties came in like a thief in the night.
It had no conscious.

Jobs now being offered to black mamas
instead of black daddies.
Now mama and daddy are both gone.
No one to care for the children-devastation at its best!
Crack cocaine hit the streets and
the making of troubled kids emerged.
Laws created: 3 Strikes You Out and
You better not discipline your children.
The prison industry growing faster than a chain of McDonalds.

Today we find many of our black families in a state of confusion.
Black daddies and mamas in prison or addicted to drugs and alcohol.
HIV+, Bipolar disorder, homelessness, and
gang banging consuming the community.
Grand mamas and family members are left raising the children.
Lord knows they are doing their best.
While foster care and juvenile court are creating a mess.

And you want to know what went wrong?
A creation of conditions that destroyed people dignity.
It was a decade of changes where individuals
fell down and never got back up.

Escape

Sometimes I have to get out of this world.
I have to escape and go far, far away.
If I do not, I may fall through the cracks of
self-destruction, manipulation, and corruption.

Perhaps, I may become unthinkingly racist,
and be swallowed up by the hatred and despair.
If I do not go, my cynical outlook on the
world may cause me to be aloof.

I may even become deranged from all the
madness I witness everyday.
Thus, I have to go—if only for an instance.
I have to escape the snarls of this world.

Although I go, I do not want to stay gone too
long. Like others, I may not find my way back.
So just for a moment, I need to get away -
far, far away. Yes, I have to escape.

Family Ideology

We have babies with the intent
to be a good mother and father.
We have babies by men we thought
we knew and perhaps, loved.
We have babies believing
we can and will do
the right thing by them and for them.
We have babies hoping to give them more love,
extra protection, and guidance.
But soon those thoughts of a happy
family fade away into the day-to-day
cycle of dysfunctional lives – issues
love itself cannot heal nor make go away.

Some think just because we have babies
out of wedlock by men who have issues of
being irresponsible, abusive, and unloving,
that we are unfit mothers.
They look at us as if we have no morals
or know the traditions of a loving family.
Though we make bad choices in men,
we still want what others have–to be a good mother
and have a loving father for our children.
We stay in those abusive and unhealthy relationships.
We do so mostly because of our family ideology.
We want our family to stay together.
We want our children to have a
mama and daddy to look up too.

Donna Reed

Perhaps, we are looked upon by many as foolish,
unstable, and unbalanced women.
But wait, sometimes our reasoning for holding
on to our baby daddies go beyond the concept of love.
Most often, we look at our kids and see ourselves
growing up without our own fathers.
We remember the pain we endured,
the anger we kept hidden, and the rejection we often felt.
And with that moment of glare, we overlook the warning signs.
We endure the mental and physical abuse.
And because we ourselves were left alone without
our fathers, we fear the abandonment for our children.
We turn our eyes upon our youngsters and we say,
our babies need their daddies.
So we stay.
We stay in hopes and prayers we can be a family.

We stay as long as we can.
For many, we stay too long–too late.
And then we have regrets.
But when you want for your child that
which you did not have, reality usually
do not set in until later.
Then we think about what we could,
should, and would have done.
And because we were believing that the
family ideology was within our reach,
we could not, did not, nor wanted to see
it was only a delusion.
And that we got caught up in the mere thoughts
of having a mama, daddy, and our sons
and daughters living together as one.

In Memory of Baby Detrick Corbett, Jr.

No Price at All

I remember being outside on a hot summer day
playing marbles for keep and hide-n-go-seek;
jumping double-dutch rope and reading the horoscopes.
And though those days are long gone,
there is no price for my memories – no price at all.

I remember swinging real high on the swings in the
early season of the Spring; sliding down the giant slide
and getting dizzy from the merry-go-ride.
And though those days are long gone,
there is no price for my memories – no price at all.

I remember dressing up on Easter Sundays and
getting a bellyache from eating the chocolate bunnies.
And oh I could not wait to find the colored boiled eggs,
for I knew one was hidden behind the front lawn hedge.
And though those days are long gone,
there is no price for my memories – no price at all.

I remember eating watermelon on the front porch
and enduring the pain from the hot summer scorch.
The late evenings were filled with catching lightning
bugs in one of my grandmama mason jugs.
And though those days are long gone,
there is no price for my memories – no price at all.

Whatever happened to those days? Where did they go?
Oh how I miss them so. I miss the joy, the innocence
they brought to my young and fervent heart.
They make me laugh. They make me cry.
They are cherished moments I cannot deny.
Memories that are embedded in my heart and soul.
They are more precious than silver and gold.
There is no price for my memories - no price at all.

Donna Reed

My Traveling Man

Tell me why are you going to and fro?
To see the world, gain new experiences.
Is it to meet new people – all sorts of people?
Giving words of encouragement;
thus causing the soul to rejoice.
Tell me is it the freedom of traveling?
Feeling attracted and affected by its
mystery, beauty, and uniqueness.
He's my traveling man, my traveling man,
Oh how I love my traveling man.

He's always on the move driven by his own
inquisitiveness and self motivation.
Traveling is a part of his life – making the
best of it even if it wasn't planned.
He believes in experiencing all he can.
He doesn't hold himself back
waiting for others to join.
I got me a cosmopolitan.
He's my traveling man, my traveling man,
Oh how I love my traveling man.

So as he goes to and fro enjoying life,
spreading happiness along the way.
Wisdom is upon him now.
Time has taught him patience.
He told me the other day,
"Baby I'm getting tired,
 I want a place I can call home."
There will never be rest for a man
that can move, move, and keep moving.
He's my traveling man, my traveling man,
Oh how I love my traveling man.

The Flight

Opening up like a wildflower
on a hot summer day,
where both natures
are craving the same.
Sliding their way through
to a comfort zone,
zippin in and out,
up and down, and around;
Obtaining that last upward
thrust and collision,
thus calling out ones destination.
Grasping and holding
on for dear life
with moments of
instant shudder and bliss.
Reeling with unfettered
joy and contentment
and being where
both had hoped to be.
Knowing either one of
them could get there–
there being anywhere
one wanted to go.

Heeey – That's All Right

Remembering you Donny

What a Star! Born rightfully so.
A sensational performer don't you know.
A man who sung with so much soul.
He makes me want to move and groove all night long.
He takes the effect of music to another level.
He makes me feel vivacious and giddy with joy.
I party with him in The Ghetto.
I cry with him in Giving Up.
With such intensity, I feel all of his inside pain.
And just like that – He makes me throw up my hands,
pop my fingers, and dance the whole song through.
He makes me want to say, Heeey – That's All Right!

What a Star! A sensational performer.
But I wonder so often about his death.
How could a young man die so gifted and unique.
He was born a star though his life has come and gone.
But Donny you are still the man because when
I listen to you, you make me drop my head, close my
eyes, and move my head from side to side and then
I holler, Heeey – That's All Right!
And I groove and party some more.

New York, I Cry

I was just there – there where I saw
buildings and skyscrapers – so many, so tall.
It was our first encounter.
You took my breath away.
A true cosmopolitan, I must indeed say.

You was everything on TV, in Hollywood and more,
I saw a real city like nothing I had seen before.
You was astonishing – a world of your own.
You filled me with awe.
Your prominence forever known.

Your power permeated with a sense of liberty.
I smiled as I hailed my first yellow taxi.
Though I felt a brush of arrogance
when I ask for directions, I did not take it
personal because it was not your reflection.

Looking at the masses,
the bright lights on Broadway,
I felt like a child on Christmas Day.
I heard voices – thrilling conversations and more,
as I stood outside of NBC Today Show.

Now as I look at the thick smoke and dust,
I do not recognize you – this is truly unjust.
I cannot believe someone would do this to you.
And though I am not a native,
it has affected me too!

Who are these evil forces that tore into our land?
Could it be a sign of end times interpreted by man?
How can this happen in America,
the home of the free? Whatever it was,
the world stood silently in disbelief!

So I cry for you, the firefighters,
victims, and rescue team.
I know it is madness in the uttermost extreme.
I cry for the buildings I cannot see anymore.
This impact has touched me down to the core.

I pray in time you will heal and stand tall.
And I hope to never see another building fall.
Though a cloud of dust may cover you now,
do not worry, you will arise someway – somehow.
You will become the mecca again, a place one yearns to go.
And my heart will be elated as I call to mind Ground Zero!

What Will I Be Tomorrow

One day I was called
an African Descendant.
Next, I was called
the masters slave.
Then I became a niggar.
While later becoming
a colored child.
Soon I became
the New Negro.
And I called myself
black and proud.
Ten years later,
I became an
African American.
And finally today,
091101
I became an
American.
But what will
I be tomorrow?

Donna Reed

Imposter

Many of us pretend to have it going on.
When in fact, we are miserable, unhappy,
discontent, full of distortions.
We do not even know who we are anymore.
We hide behind trendy fads, broken families
and homes, conditional love, inadequate finances,
and habitual forces embedded throughout
a child life, thus becoming a vicious cycle.

Whatever happened to being true to one self?
Whatever happened to the fundamentals of life?
Whatever happened to knowing who you are?
I say we are beyond being one of the stepford wives.
We are close to becoming clones.

So I say to the Imposter,
beware of the tales you tell yourself.
Beware of the narration you hear from others.
Look into the mirror.
You will see the real true person.
Why continue to impersonate?
When you can be your own natural make!

Is It Me

I want to know my brother have time
brought about a change?
We don't greet and communicate with one another.
What happened to being friends–hanging out–
laughing about old school?
Tell me my brother, is it your environment that
makes you so uneasy or is it me?
I see a change in you. It did not use to be this way.

When I see you sitting at the lunch table,
I want to come and sit with you.
Perhaps talk about your kids, my kids, politics, and sports.
I suppose you are afraid of what others may think.
But why is it if you sit with me, we have to be intimate.
Tell me my brother, is it your environment that
makes you so uneasy or is it me?
I see a change in you. It did not use to be this way.

As I observed you dressed in your suit and tie and
working hard for your money,
I want to say you are one classy guy.
But I know scandal and sexual harassment have
spread itself in the minds of many of you.
Just know I am not trying to destroy you or your profession.
I just want to say I am proud of you.
So tell me my brother, is it your environment that
makes you so uneasy or is it me?
I see a change in you. It did not use to be this way.

But I long for the day we can be brothers and sisters again.
I wait with anticipation–I wait!

Five Long Days

First day,
I was afraid
of what I saw,
mighty winds and
rain and gushing
water to no end.

Second day,
I cried for the souls
and the city.
The water was still rising.
I became horrified.

Third day,
I was still crying
and waiting for my government
to send help and rescue the people.

I saw on CNN,
the Civic Center,
Superdome and those
stranded on their rooftops.
I saw babies dressed
in nothing but their diapers.

I saw men and women
crying desperately,
toddlers and children
of all ages bewildered.
I saw the elderly slouched
over in wheelchairs.

I saw the sick,
the lame, and feeble.
I saw my people.
I saw the poor.
I saw those who could not leave
because they had no means.

Fourth day,
I got mad and yelled,
"Wait a minute,
where the hell is help?
Where is our national guard?
The city is under water for God sake!"

Then I heard the people say,
"No food, No water,
No medicine
in three days!"
I became irate and
cursed at the TV news.

Fifth day,
I was disgusted with
my government and politics.
And I cried,
Lord help my people
to survive this nightmare!

And the world saw
along with me those whom
had been forgotten and
those who were downtrodden.

Hold Tight

Do not ever let go of your dreams.
Hold tight.
Just know, shit happens.
But you are resilient and
known through mankind
to bounce back and you will.
Had you not gone there,
you would not be who you are now.
Had you not gone through it,
you would not be where you are today.

More often than not,
our dreams should be a better life for
our children and future generations.
They are our future. Everything else is futile.
And despite our own issues,
we have to break the cycle of
self-destruction – impediments that are keeping
our children from living healthy and normal lives.
Hold tight and do not ever let go.

That is why you cannot let anyone take
your dreams away; for they may be taking
away the dreams of your children and
perhaps, the next generation.
And if you can look into the mirror
and then look into the eyes of your son
and daughter. You will see the bigger
picture – and that is, their dreams
can be far bigger than your own!
Remember when we let go,
we give up on ourselves and we
let our sons and daughters down.
Hold tight and do not ever let go.

I Could Paint a Pretty Picture

I could paint a pretty picture and
no one would know the truth.
Not my father, mother, brother or sister.
Not even my many friends nor my lover.
I could even fool myself into believing
I was whole, healthy, and at peace.
You see I had become an expert at painting a pretty picture.

It was not until those lurking demons revisited me
on more than one occasion—demons I thought
I had out-smarted and out-grew.
Sometimes I escaped them via man escape plan.
Other times I covered them up—you know painting
the marks and scars to the perfect blend.

I even tried to fight back and lost to no avail.
I suddenly realized they were much bigger and
stronger than me—too big for me to fight alone.
They stripped me—uncovered the beauty I had
displayed outwardly. They brought me shame
and disgrace that made me want to hide and run away.

I cried out, please leave me alone!
They called me names: Hypocrite! Imposter! Liar!
I covered my ears but they got louder.
I need healing, healing I cannot do alone.
I was tired of running and hiding my inner pain.
I was sick and tired of me—the one who was
the master of painting a pretty picture.

Donna Reed

Epitome of a Mother

You sacrificed your pride for carrying me
in your belly as an unwed mother.

You sacrificed your talent, a true contralto, and gave up your dream
because you could not leave me behind.

You washed and ironed dirty clothes, pressed and curled
nappy hair to earn a dollar to provide for me.

You stood on your aching feet ten hours a day
to move me out of the ghetto.

You prayed for me and gave me over to the Lord
when you knew not what to do.

You drove hundreds of miles to see about me
when I faced turmoil in my troubled marriage.

You welcomed my children and I back home
when we did not have anywhere else to go.

As long as I can remember–you made sacrifices for me
and I can never ever thank you enough.

I know my life would not be what it is today
had it not been for a mother like you.

You are a true Matriarch–so full of grace.
You dignity is such a powerful force.
Your faith is stalwart.
You are the epitome of a mother!

I Am

There have been moments in my life
I didn't know myself.
There have been days I wasn't proud
of the person I was.
But today I choose to accept who and what I am.
I chose today to change my thinking.
I am creating my reality every minute, everyday.
I chose now to know myself as these things.

I am goodness.
I am compassion.
I am understanding.
I am forgiving.
I am peace.
I am joy.
I am beautiful.
I am these things.

There have been days where I thought
material things would make me whole.
There have been days when everyone and
everything around me felt temporary and fragile.
But today I choose to accept who and what I am.
I chose today to change my thinking.
I am creating my reality every minute, everyday.
I chose now to know myself as these things.

I am goodness.
I am compassion.
I am understanding.
I am forgiving.
I am peace.
I am joy.
I am beautiful.
I am these things.

Donna Reed

I Say To You, Sara Live

Embrace this time girl,
soon it will be no more.
Look at you–gorgeous–a knock-out,
one of those got-it-going-on
sisters from old school.
I say to you, Sara live.

Embrace the good times.
Let the negative events go.
Pretty soon you will have
only memories and you want
those memories to be all good!
I say to you, Sara live.

Appreciate, love and be kind to yourself.
If you look closely, you will see
you have plenty of good inside of you.
And remember, you only have one
life and then you're gone.
So I say to you, Sara live.

I Want a Black Man

I want a black man, a man of my dreams.

I want his eyes to look at me as if I am the only one.

I want his winning smile to brighten up my days.

I want his luscious lips to kiss me softly again and again.

I want his ears to hear me when I speak and cry.

I want his strong broad shoulders to lay my head upon.

I want his muscular arms to catch me when I am falling.

I want his firm hands to gently stroke my face.

I want his legs to hold me when I sit upon his lap.

I want his feet to walk side by side with me.

I want his heart to beat to the rhythm of mine.

All things considered,

I want a black man – a man of my dreams.

Donna Reed

Life Is Worth Living

Life is worth living.
Seeing her in her electronic wheelchair,
she was smiling and talking to her friends.
I looked up and said life is worth living.

As I watched her enter the door and ride
on to class, I admired her strength and her
determination to get an education in spite of
her conditions. Her magnetic force reached
out and touched me in a way I will never forget.
With admiration, I smiled.

It does not matter if you are missing a limb.
It does not matter if you are confine to a
wheelchair or have some other disability.
What matters is that you know life is worth
living in spite of the conditions that surround
you or the obstacles that come before you.

And whenever I find myself feeling like life is
unfair, I remember the young lady in the
wheelchair. It was her attitude. It was her
respect for herself, her personal honor and
integrity that resonated from her system.
It was her appreciation for life. She reminded
me life is worth living.

Little Miss Briana

Little Miss Briana,
a child that had so much life.
Your eyes brimmed with joy.
But on a cold, clear Christmas Day,
the angels came and took you away.
Your untimely demise is etched
with sorrow, but we know you
are resting in the bosom of our Father.

Little Miss Briana,
If we could have saved you
we would have. But there
was nothing anyone could do.
We even wonder what could
we have done differently
to save you from the pain.
But as we look back,
it is not too much we
could have done if the
circumstances that were
surrounding our lives at the
time were the same.

Little Miss Briana,
it is so hard to hold back the tears,
but we know time will heal our
broken hearts.
Time will bring us
peace and comfort.
And although time has brought
us pain and sorrow,
we know time has a way of
bringing us joy once again.

In Memory of Briana Lancaster

Donna Reed

Long Lost Reunion

A Father and his Child

I saw you in my dream last night.
It was one I did not want to wake up from.
We hugged, laughed, and talked.
What a reunion! I felt like a precious stone.
I thought why could my days as a child been like this.
You apologized for your absence and I forgave you likewise.

As I looked into your eyes, I saw my own.
The shape of your brow, mouth, and round face
all look like me! Without a doubt, I was indeed your child.
For a moment, I awaken and realized it was just a dream.
I was hoping to resume as I drifted back to sleep.
And there you was standing and waiting to give
me one more big hug. I smiled. I saw you no more.

Though you were gone, I felt good.
It was just like a long lost reunion
between a father and his child.
I even remembered your birthday
being in the month of July.
And I wondered did you remember the day I was born.
Although we were cheated out of a relationship together,
I was made strong and survived your absence.

I have grown to understand why you were not there.
I have come to grips knowing it was not all your error.
Sometimes kids are forced into situations
by life unfortunate circumstances.
And so it is, I can not change the bloodlines nor the
strong genes, and sweet tooth that were passed down
from you to me. And so it is, you are my father and
you will always be!

Mama Hicks

Mama Hicks, the mother of all.
You were there when I needed you most.
A young mother needing to be shown the
right way – how to be a mother.
Oh, I learned and gained so much from you!

I thank you for helping me, a new mother
trying to raise a child for the first time, alone.
I want you to know while working,
I never worried one bit because it
was you taking care of my baby.

You showed me how to feed her and wean
her from the bottle. You told me how to give
her honey each morning to keep away the ear
aches and colds. You even taught me how to
be stern and gain respect along the way.

Mama Hicks it was you who opened up
your heart and home. You became my guide.
And for that, I want to say thank you.
Thank you for showing me the way.
Thank you for showing me how to be a mother.

Donna Reed

My Baby

I remember the day I brought you home from the hospital.
You were the center of attention and all eyes were on you.
You were a perfect baby, a beautiful baby, a good baby.
But most important, you were my baby.

As I watched you grow into being a little girl,
I myself was growing making mistakes along the way.
However, your constant love assured me that you was
there for me like I was there for you.
But most important, you were still my little girl.

As days passed by and months turned into years,
I saw you develop into a little lady.
With changing hormones and flaring attitudes,
it overwhelmed me – you were no longer my little baby.
By the grace of God, we both made it through.
But still and most important, you were my little lady.

And now when I look at you all grown up,
I smile just as I did the day you were born.
No mother can be as proud as I am today because
you have turned out to be a beautiful young lady.

May God continue to bless you just as I know He will do
because you and I both know prayer will see you through.
So as you take your first journey into the world,
always remember I am right here and I will always care.

And just to let you know, all eyes are still on you.
The same as they were when you could barely coo.
So here is to my daughter, my little girl, my little lady,
but far most important, here is to my baby!

Friend for Life

I remember the day we met:
Two souls whose lives were
parallel undeniably so.
Your spirit – gentle as a lamb,
humane as Mother Theresa
resonated across the room.
I happily admired your wit.
You made me stop crying long
enough to belly laugh.
God must have known
I needed to express mirth.
You are nothing but an
angel sent from above.

Who would have thought a girl
from Texas and a girl from Tennessee
would come together and help each
other do and be all we can be.
Though many miles have separated us now,
I know you are only a phone call away.
Indeed our lives intertwine and we share a
bond only the Lord could have formed.
You are my friend for life.

Donna Reed

My Leader – My Angel

I remember the day you were born – so complete.
The last of the ice and snow had disappeared,
grasses were growing green.
No doubt, you was predestined to be here.
You are my leader, my angel from above.

You lead me to make the right decisions as I carried
you for nine months. You kicked and stretched
so much until I thought you was an active little boy.
I was lead to believe that until the day you was born.
You are my leader, my angel from above.

You are so energetic and full of life.
Even in the womb, you lead and I followed.
You possess such leadership qualities.
You are my own little president.
You are my leader, my angel from above.

Your look of content–
your attitude of I can,
inspires me each and every day.
I am so glad for the day you were born.
You are my leader, my angel from above.

Children of all ages have come running and
asking where are you. That is a special gift.
Perhaps one day you will become a charismatic leader.
But until then, as I watch you grow and develop,
you are my leader, my angel from above.

Oh America

Oh America, Oh, America!
When will you be what you say you are?
The Land of Democracy – The Land of Opportunity.
Time after time you have proven to be an
institution refusing to move forward in unity.

Oh America, Oh America!
When will you recognize the growing
diversity residing in your land?
Because until you do,
You cannot and will not stand.

Oh America, Oh America!
Can you see the citizens are willing
to fight for justice and equality.
But if you continue to influence your ideologies,
one day you will fall and remember your irregularities.

Oh America, Oh America!
The world is watching you.
But knowing you – you will ignore it like you always do.
And then and only then the world will see you are
nothing more than an institution full of hypocrisy!

Tell me America,
when will you be what you say you are to me?

Donna Reed

Our Forefathers

Do we live in such different worlds
that we do not feel the same pain when a love one dies
or feel the same joy when a child is born?

Do we not bleed the same when we are cut by a knife or
paper cut? Or function by the same organs and limbs?
Do we not all cry because of fear, pain, sadness, and joy?
Were we not born the same way via the womb of a mother?

Do not our bodies grow old and then we die?
Do that make us different or do it make us the same?
Could it be we are dissimilar because of a system
of social deference – a system of segregation?

Have old laws caused people to perceive themselves
to be better than others? Is it because of the notion of
white superiority and black deferiority? All legitimated through
community approval; and all triggered by provincialism,
poverty, caste gains and solidarity.

Could this be why we live in a world of biases,
prejudices, and wrongful treatment towards one another?
Could these attitudes be that of history?

What is sown in a nation will eventually uproot itself.
If none of the latter ever existed, would we be the same?
After all are we not all human beings? Our world is
suffering and will continue to do so because of our forefathers.

Prodigal Girl

I was spiritually dying and,
I did not even know it.
I knew something was wrong when I went
to church and left the same way as I came,
Burden Down.

I remember blaming the preacher for
not feeding my hunger appetite.
I did not understand why I felt so alone.
I found myself weeping throughout the nights.
The feeling of despair was visiting me
more often than not.

I suppose I could say the task of
parenting alone,
obtaining an education,
and working full time
became my crux.
I got caught up in surviving.
I do not remember when it all began.
But it was a gradual process,
something unnoticeable.

I remember my first spiritual
awakening many years ago.
It was a high that marijuana, cocaine, and
hennessy could not touch.
It was a freedom like that of Mandela.
I felt I could soar like an eagle.

I was praying in the spirit,
seeing in the spirit,
and dancing in the spirit.
And even though life at the time was
troublesome, I had peace like a river.

But here I was at a locale
I had not journeyed before.
I never imagined I could end up in
the very place as the Prodigal boy.
I felt empty – I felt lost.
My cupboard had become bare.

I longed for a touch – a whisper in my ear.
I wanted my cup to run over.
I needed my soul to be revived.
I just wanted to fellowship with
my Father like old times.

I knew it was the hour for me to return
to the place in which I had been born.
So I called my Father.
I told him I wanted to come home.
I asked him to please wait for me at the door.

And so He did.
With arms wide open,
he welcomed me back home.
There I sensed a tide of joy washing over me.
My soul was glad – my soul was made glad indeed!

Slave Driven

When you do what they want,
you are their prize possession.
When you fail them,
you are cast aside.

They punish you with their
stares – whispers – halfass smiles.
And you are afraid because
of the unknown.

One day you are their heroes.
The next day you are the enemy.
And the rain falls on the just
as well as the unjust.

When you win,
it is a celebration.
It brings about rewards
and compensations.

When you lose,
it is someone fault.
It brings about fines
and retributions.

Donna Reed

Something To Be Valued

Sons and daughters
what are you going to do now
that you do not go to school?
Is it a pervasive sense of
hopelessness?

What are you going to say when
life passes you by? And who
are you going to blame when you
become an underclassman?

Why are you giving up my child?
Why are you throwing in the towel?
Do you not know an education
is something to be valued!

Without it, you have no pride.
Without it, doors will be closed.
Perhaps, find yourselves among the suffering.
Perhaps, find yourselves behind prison bars.

So tell me sons and daughters
what are you going to do
to better yourselves–better your lives?
Please tell me you are going back to school!

The Bigger Picture

She always had him to look at the bigger picture.
She reminded him to always cherish his children.
And so he did.
He changed for the sake of his kids.
He ended the cycle of self-destruction
that has run rampant in his family.
She made him remember who he was
and how far he had come.
She reminded him that he was
a black man in America.
She told him not only was he strong,
but he was strong for his sons and daughters.
And so he stood up as a man
and made a commitment to
cultivate his children, especially
his own little black boys and girls.
He saw the bigger picture!

Johnson

I know I said I am finished with Johnson.
I know I said I am not going to call him anymore.
I know I said I am tired of him controlling
my mind, body, and soul.

Although he makes me do things I know are irresponsible,
many times overpowered by his strength and compulsivity.
Johnson soothes the urges and anxieties that grab
a hold of me. He satisfies the nights I am alone.
He makes me feel wholesome–he makes me feel anew.

I know I said I am finished with Johnson.
But today he called my name and I found
myself running to him with arms wide open.
I went running only to find myself empty–
only to find myself empty once again.

Although I crave him, I can not have him when
I want him. That is difficult for me.
That is difficult for any unsatisfied craving.
No doubt, I am addicted to Johnson.

I know I said I am finished with Johnson.
Right now I am.
He may call tomorrow and I cannot tell
you how I am going to respond.
I do know it is hard to say no to him.
And it is so easy to say yes.

Indeed Johnson is crafty and effective.
Johnson is strong and regal.
You cannot pretend he does not exist.
Indeed, Johnson is real!

The Birds and Bees

Not an hour goes by that I do not think of you.
I dissolve at your touch.
You warm me when I am cold.
Heat wave sweeps into my belly.
You soothes me when I am distressed.
I ache with an inner longing.
You take me places I have not gone before.
I grow feverish with desire.
You set my blood aflame.
My toes curl in ecstasy.
Your power is phenomenal.
You breathe words of desire.
You make me do crazy things.
That is why not an hour goes by
I do not think of you.
I cannot help but smile!
I cannot help but laugh out loud!
hahahahahaha...................

The Color of Skin

How long Oh Lord must we struggle and fight?
Everyday we wake up – we are reminded that we are black.
We are reminded in our schools, in our churches, on our jobs,
in our prisons and courtrooms.

We are reminded in every poverty-stricken neighborhood to
the most influential suburb. We are reminded across the airwaves,
television stations, and newspapers. We are even reminded
surfing the internet.

Tell me Lord why are we being punished because of the color
of our skin? All we ever asked for was to be given a fair chance.
Although we are proud of our heritage and who we are, we did
not ask to be born with differences that separate us from others.

It is us whose skin color determines the outcome of their life.
We did not choose to be black and live such life.
For so many years, we have been fighting for our
civil rights, our dignity, and pride.

All we want is to be treated like human beings. People have
lost their lives because of the color of their skin.
We are judged, stereotyped, and critiqued everyday we live.
What more could we possibly give?

I just want to know why my people have been dealt such a hand.
We cannot help who we are! Lord you made us and placed us in
this land!

The Odds

When the odds are against them,
how do they do it?

When the family is torn apart,
how can they have stability?

When their childhood was beyond dysfunctional,
how can they become productive adults?

When they do not know how,
how can they raise healthy babies?

When they do not have the means,
how can they be real fathers and mothers?

When the odds are against them,
tell me how can it be done?

Donna Reed

The Wounded Child

We have lost our damn minds!
We are hurting each other – constantly.
Tearing down each other spirits purposely.
There was a time when we cried with one another,
laughed together, and leaned on one another.
Needless to say, we do not do that anymore.

Now we have become estrange– remote–cold and lonely.
So many of our hearts have been broken and damaged
until we are afraid of opening our hearts again.
But who knows our soul mate may come
along and because of the wounded child that lies
within us, we allow that soul mate to pass us by.

We are so caught up with trying to survive that
we forget what matters most: our children and each other.
We cannot extend a hand because we ourselves need help.
Within each of us, there lies the wounded child:
painful memories, negative attitudes, and dysfunctional
self-images. We become the frightened child trying to walk
among a world of constant change and disappointment.

But we got to do the necessary work to help us heal so
we can lie our heads on each other shoulders and cry
if need be. We must do the work that is vital
to our lives and to the lives of our children.
We must do what we can to win the game of life.
Don't you see we really do need each other in this
sometimes cruel, cruel world!

Time

Today my heart is heavy.
I feel like I have come to an intersection
and I do not know which way to go.

I am looking both ways, yet I am
confused on whether to take a
left or right turn or go straight.

I want to hear an audible voice speak.
I keep listening and expecting to hear,
but there is no sound.

I know what I want and where I want to go.
But I am still trying to read the map.
How can I get there? How can I make it happen?

When life turmoil stares me in the face,
I have learned nothing can unravel it but time.

Time is the essence.
Time takes care of everything.
You cannot rush it or slow it down.
Just let it be.

If I can wait and let time come to my rescue.
Then all of my wants will be there
and I will find my way.

With time I will obtain my wants.
With certainty I will find my way.
Because time is the source of strength
and it always brings change!

Donna Reed

Valentine's Day

The day is just two weeks away.
And already we are beginning to panic.
Our heart flutters.
That unwretched feeling of fear
residing in the pits of our belly.
Will I get red roses or flowers?
Will I get a romantic dinner or hot sex?
Will I get to be with the one I love?

But why ask those questions when
you should know all of the above.
On any given day, a man should give
his lady red roses. At any given time,
a woman should give her man some good lovin'.
Do we not understand the fundamentals?

The pressure is on the brother
to do what is popular–do what is right.
He runs. He hides. He is confused.
Turmoil within makes it hard for him to think,
but he manages to escape it all.
He goes into seclusion.
No phone calls. No cards.
No candy. No flowers.

The pressure is on the sister.
She wants a date–a fine wine–a good lay.
She wants to be with the one she loves.
Although she loves him, she wonders
if he loves her the same.
She anxiously waits to see if she is the special one.
Throughout the night, she waits in silence,
then in anger, but mostly in grief and disappointment.

The day is just two weeks away.
And already we are beginning to panic.
Our heart flutters.
That unwretched feeling of fear
residing in the pits of our belly.
Will I get red roses or flowers?
Will I get a romantic dinner or hot sex?
Will I get to be with the one I love?

But why ask those questions when
you should know all of the above.
On any given day, a man should give
his lady red roses. At any given time,
a woman should give her man some good lovin'.
Do we not understand the fundamentals?

The pressure is on the husbands and wives.
Poor wives, at least some,
wait to see if she is still the mate,
for better-for worse; for richer-for poorer.
Girlfriends think the coochie is platinum,
and she uses it to break up a happy home.
Soon she wants the unattainable:
She wants the husband to be in love
with her instead of the wife.

Valentine's Day is the big day.
But many of us know we will not be getting anything.
We condition our minds to believe it is just another day.
We front as if it do not bother us to be alone.
But sure it does. If you do not have a date,
society says something is wrong.
And we are alone until next year when
Valentine's Day rolls around again.
And the cycle continues the same........

Where I Need To Be

I do not like where I am, but I know I am
where the Creator wants me to be.
I yearn to go back to grabbing a shot
of Jack, inhaling a smoke or two, and
perhaps going over the mountain.
But I will not go back there because
I know I am where I need to be.

The Creator is dealing with me now.
He is healing my mind, body, and soul.
If I plan to move forward in life,
I must stay here and allow Him to
work with me and my wounds–
wounds which have lead to my fears.
And so I cannot go back and I will not
because I know this is where I need to be.

Undoubtedly the battle is difficult, the
most formidable opposition of my life.
But if I expect to win the war, I cannot
pretend the issues are not real or the
addictions do not exist. Disavowal can
cost me my life. Therefore, I must
stay here, right here in this
uncomfortable and unfamiliar place.

A Blessed Man

My brother is a blessed man.
One of the best guys one can know.
A man with so many hats.
Smart and intelligent too!
He's suave as a runway model.
Looking like Brooks Brothers on any given day.
His debonair walk diverted by his own wit.
His buoyant personality made him friends for life.
His bel-air smile puts you at ease.
Anyone would appreciate his great sense of humor.

My brother is a blessed man.
One of the best guys one can know.
A family man - devout husband.
I'm so proud of the way he's being
a father to his son and daughter.
When they are in his presence,
their bright eyes brim with joy!
They skip and hop all around him.
His love for his family is to no end.

My brother is a blessed man.
One of the best guys one can know.
His picky eating habits,
good work ethics,
and love for sports,
make him undeniably special!
He's a role model to the truest measure.
He's been a positive figure for my own children.
He's a man that stands by his word.
He's a man who believes in the Highest!

Family & Friends

These are the ones who are there when we need them most.
Without our family and friends,
our lives are incomplete.
We watch each other grow and make mistakes.
We laugh.
We cry.
We fight.
We share each other heartaches and pains.
When there is joy and wealth,
we want to spread it among our family and friends,
whom we love – we share.
In difficult times,
we need each other to lean upon.
When we are weak,
our love ones are stalwart.
When they are helpless,
we are made mighty.
So many obstacles have come against the family,
thus causing so many families to stray apart.
And we wonder why there is so much ailing in the world.
I long for the day families come back together.
Perhaps live under the same roof so the
support base will not be hollow.